CAMBRIDGE PRIMARY
Science

Challenge

3

Jon Board and Alan Cross

CAMBRIDGE
UNIVERSITY PRESS

University Printing House, Cambridge CB2 8BS, United Kingdom

One Liberty Plaza, 20th Floor, New York, NY 10006, USA

477 Williamstown Road, Port Melbourne, VIC 3207, Australia

4843/24, 2nd Floor, Ansari Road, Daryaganj, Delhi – 110002, India

79 Anson Road, #06–04/06, Singapore 079906

Cambridge University Press is part of the University of Cambridge.

It furthers the University's mission by disseminating knowledge in the pursuit of education, learning and research at the highest international levels of excellence.

Information on this title: education.cambridge.org

First published 2016
20 19 18 17 16 15 14 13 12 11 10 9 8

Produced for Cambridge University Press by
White-Thomson Publishing
www.wtpub.co.uk

Editor: Rachel Minay
Designer: Clare Nicholas

Printed in Malaysia by Vivar Printing

A catalogue record for this publication is available from the British Library

ISBN 978-1-316-61117-3 -Paperback

Cover artwork: Bill Bolton

Contents

Introduction

This series of primary science activity books complements *Cambridge Primary Science* and progresses, through practice, learner confidence and depth of knowledge in the skills of scientific enquiry (SE) and key scientific vocabulary and concepts. These activity books will:

- enhance and extend learners' scientific knowledge and facts
- promote scientific enquiry skills and learning in order to think like a scientist
- advance each learner's knowledge and use of scientific vocabulary and concepts in their correct context.

The *Challenge* activity books extend learners' understanding of the main curriculum, providing an opportunity to increase the depth of their knowledge and scientific enquiry skills from a key selection of topics. This workbook does not cover all of the curriculum framework content for this stage.

How to use the activity books

These activity books have been designed for use by individual learners, either in the classroom or at home. As teachers and as parents, you can decide how and when they are used by your learner to best improve their progress. The *Challenge* activity books target specific topics (lessons) from Grades 1–6 from all the units covered in *Cambridge Primary Science*. This targeted approach has been carefully designed to consolidate topics where help is most needed.

How to use the units

Unit introduction

Each unit starts with an introduction for you as the teacher or parent. It clearly sets out which topics are covered in the unit and the learning objectives of the activities in each section. This is where you can work with learners to select all, most or just one of the sections according to individual needs.

The introduction also provides advice and tips on how best to support the learner in the skills of scientific enquiry and in the practice of key scientific vocabulary.

Sections

Each section matches a corresponding lesson in the main series. Sections contain write-in activities that are supported by:

- Key words – key vocabulary for the topic, also highlighted in bold in the sections
- Key facts – a short fact to support the activities where relevant
- Look and learn – where needed, activities are supported with scientific exemplars for extra support of how to treat a concept or scientific method
- Remember – tips for the learner to steer them in the right direction.

How to approach the write-in activities

Teachers and parents are advised to provide students with a blank A5 notebook at the start of each grade for learners to use alongside these activity books. Most activities will provide enough space for the answers required. However, some learner responses – especially to enquiry-type questions – may require more space for notes. Keeping notes and plans models how scientists work and encourages learners to explore and record their thinking, leaving the activity books for the final, more focused answers.

Think about it questions

Each unit also contains some questions for discussion at home with parents, or at school. Although learners will record the outcomes of their discussions in the activity book, these questions are intended to encourage the students to think more deeply.

Self-assessment

Each section in the unit ends with a self-assessment opportunity for learners: empty circles with short learning statements. Teachers or parents can ask learners to complete the circles in a number of ways, depending on their age and preference, e.g. with faces, traffic light colours or numbers. The completed self-assessments provide teachers with a clearer understanding of how best to progress and support individual learners.

Glossary of key words and concepts

At the end of each activity book there is a glossary of key scientific words and concepts arranged by unit. Learners are regularly reminded to practise saying these words out loud and in sentences to improve communication skills in scientific literacy.

1 Looking after plants

The unit challenge

The activities in this Challenge unit will extend learners' knowledge of the following topics in the Learner's Book and Activity Book:

Topic	In this topic, learners will:
1.1 Plants and their parts	see Skills Builder, Section 1.1
1.2 Plants need light and water	learn that plants need light and water
1.3 Transporting water	see Skills Builder, Section 1.3
1.4 Plant growth and temperature	learn that most plants grow best when it is warm

Help your learner

In this unit, learners will practise measuring using simple equipment and recording observations (Section 1.2). They will also draw conclusions from evidence and begin to use scientific knowledge to suggest explanations (Section 1.4). To help them:

1 Encourage learners to grow a young plant and measure and record its height every few days. Help them to observe the changes in the plant carefully as it grows. Draw pictures or take photographs to help see the differences.

2 Help learners to look in the local area for more evidence about how plants grow in different conditions.

TEACHING TIP

Ask learners to practise making measurements. They could measure the height of other plants and the temperature in different places or at different times of day.

1.2 Plants need light and water

measure, growth, plant, height, light, water

Plant growth

Resources
You will need a ruler.

Remember:
Remember to measure from the soil to the top of the plant.

Look at this plant growing.

1 Use a ruler to **measure** the **growth** of the **plant** each day.

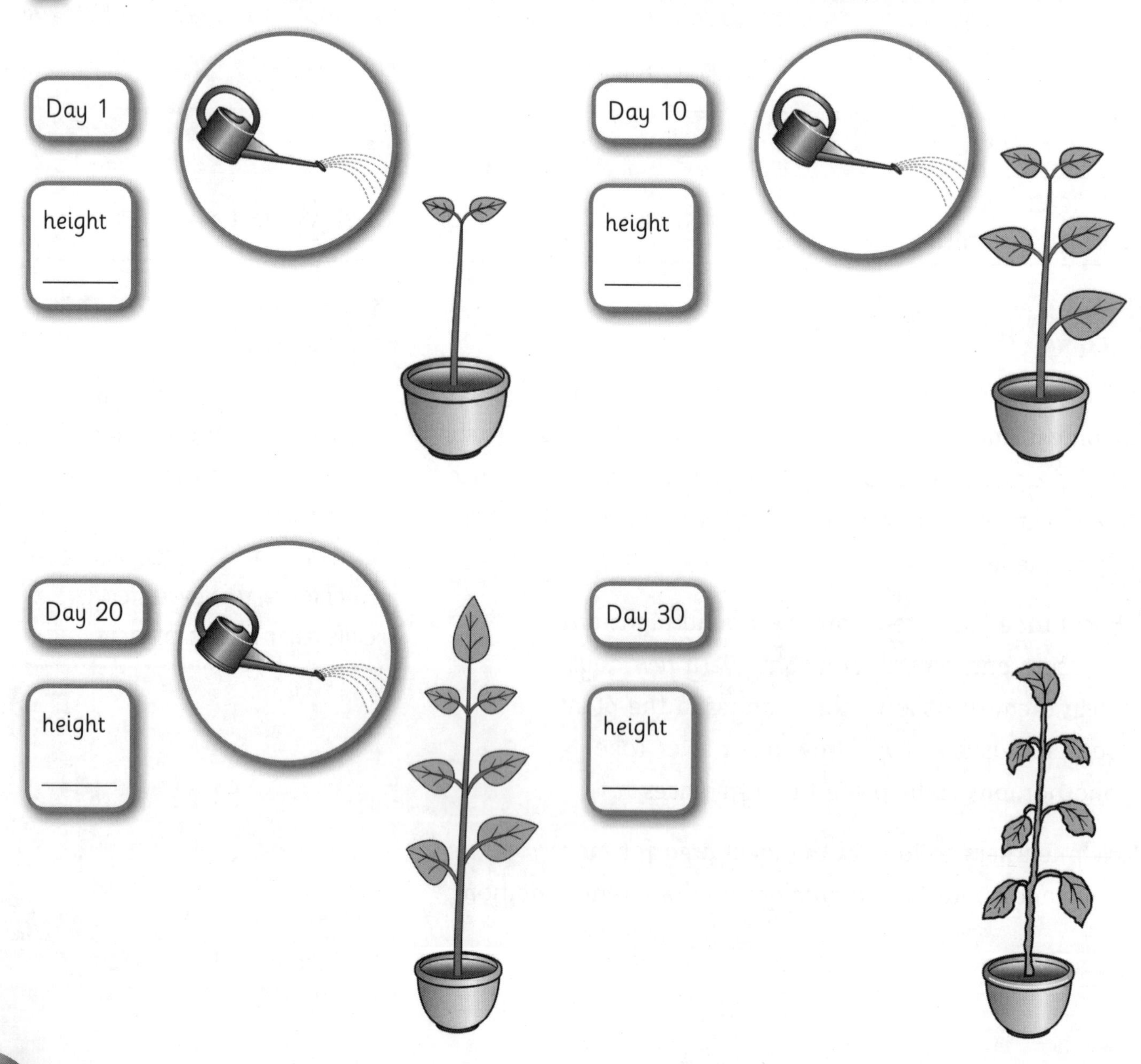

2 How many centimetres did the plant grow from day 10 to day 20?

____

3 What happened to the number of leaves as the plant grew?

____

____

4 Why do you think the plant is smaller on day 30?

____

____

5 What does the plant need to keep it alive?

____

6 **Think about it!**

Why do you think plants grow taller in the dark?

____

____

CHECK YOUR LEARNING

- ◯ I can measure **height** carefully.
- ◯ I know that plants need **light** and **water**.

1.4 Plant growth and temperature

temperature, hot, cold, roots, absorb, warm

The best place for plants

1 Where is the best place to grow these plants? Why?

____

____

2 What can you use to measure **temperature**?

____

3 What happens to plants that are too **hot** or too **cold**?

____

4 **Think about it!**

Why is it hard for **roots** to **absorb** water when it is very cold? (Clue: What happens to water when it is very cold?)

____

____

CHECK YOUR LEARNING

○ I know that most plants grow best when they are **warm**.

2 Looking after ourselves

The unit challenge

The activities in this Challenge unit will extend learners' knowledge of the following topics from the Learner's Book and Activity Book:

Topic	In this topic, learners will:
2.1 Food groups	find out more about a balanced diet
2.2 A healthy diet	understand more about healthy food
2.3 An unhealthy diet	understand that too much sugar is bad for our teeth and explore why salt can be unhealthy
2.4 Exercise and sleep	know why exercise is good for us

Help your learner

In this unit, learners will practise collecting evidence (Sections 2.2 and 2.3), making predictions (Section 2.4), presenting results, drawing conclusions and beginning to use scientific knowledge to suggest explanations (Section 2.3). To help them:

1 Remind your learner to read the headings on a table carefully and check their answers by repeating the calculations (Section 2.3).

2 Discuss the difference between a guess and a prediction: in science a prediction is an informed statement about the likely outcome, based on previous experience or knowledge.

3 When measuring seconds on a timer in Section 2.4, remind your learner to read the stopwatch carefully. Check that they understand the markings on a clock.

TEACHING TIP

Talk about what learners already know about a healthy diet and the other ways we stay healthy.

2.1 Food groups

food group, healthy, carbohydrate, fruit and vegetables, dairy, protein, fat and sugar, balanced diet

A balanced diet

1 Can you identify the five **food groups** on the **healthy** eating plate below? Use the key words to help you fill in the labels.

Remember:

A **balanced diet** includes the right amount of each food group.

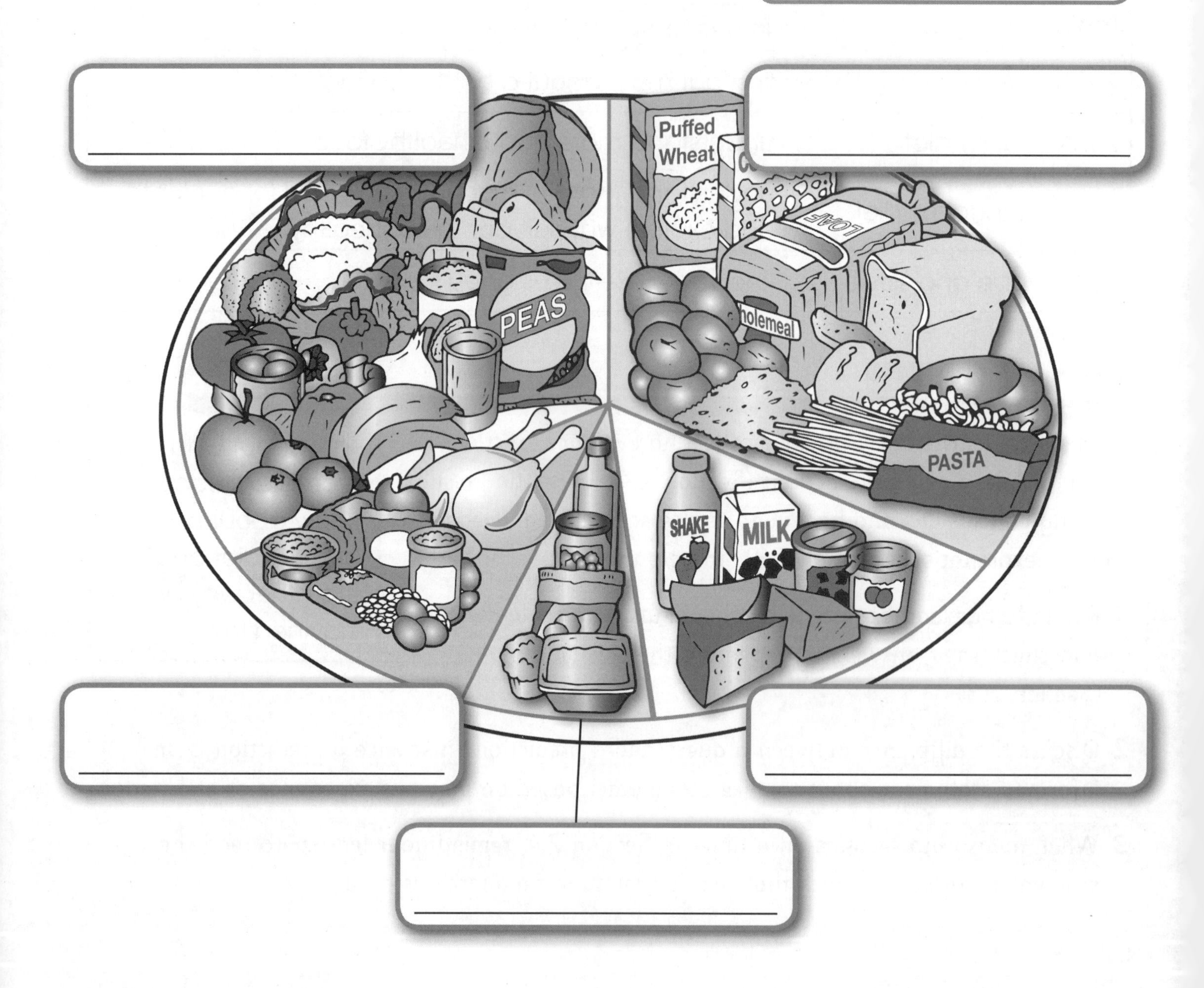

2 Sima loves fruit, sweets and cheese. Design a healthy balanced lunch for her.

3 Sam loves meat and fruit. Design a healthy balanced lunch for him.

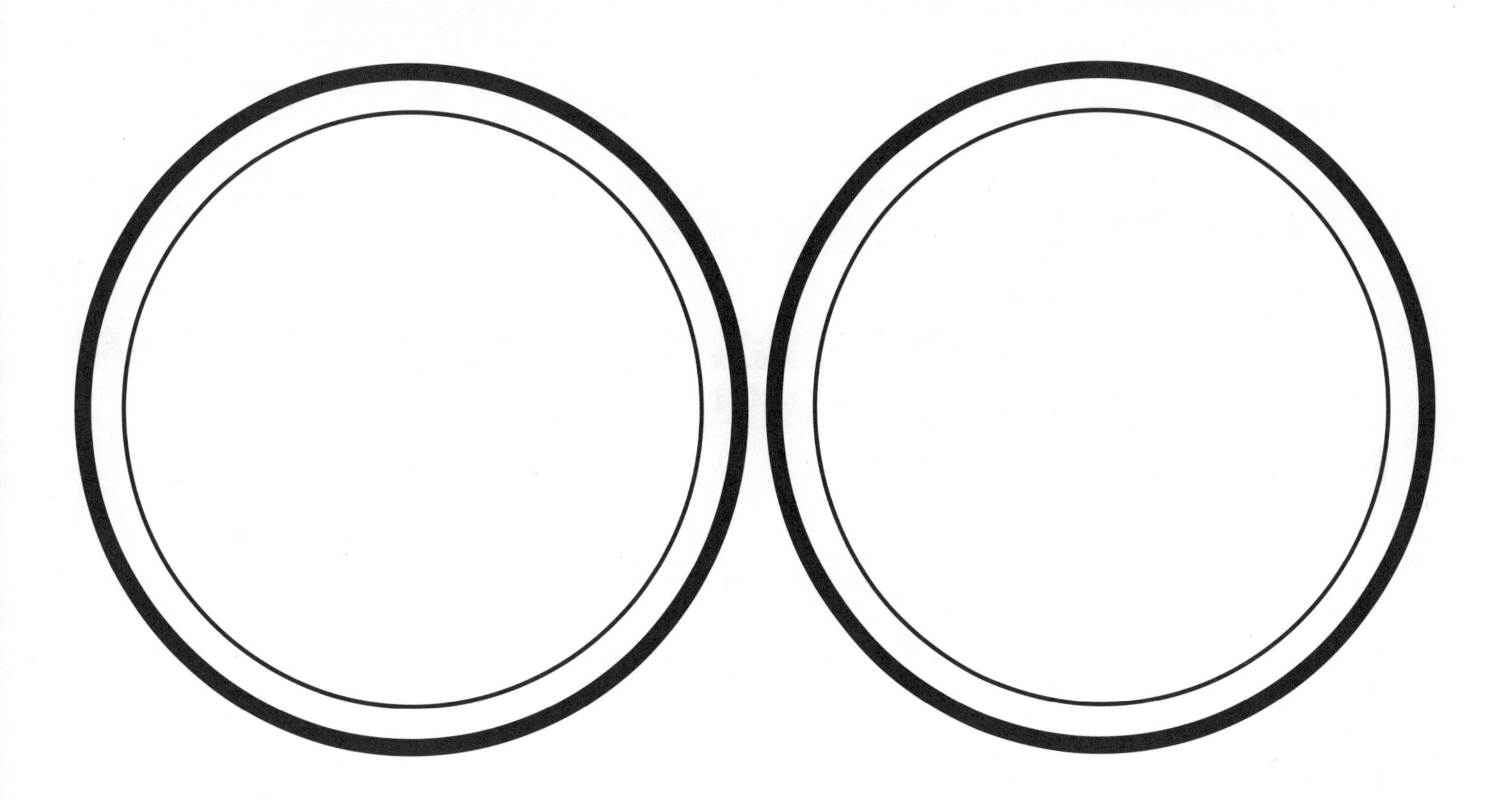

4 **Think about it!**

Which food groups do many children love? What advice would you give to your friends about the amounts to eat?

___

___

CHECK YOUR LEARNING

- I can name the five food groups.
- I can suggest ways to make a meal balanced.

added sugar, unhealthy

Healthy or treat?

Lots of healthy foods have sugar in them naturally but some foods contain added sugar.

Remember:

Remember that eating foods with lots of added sugar is **unhealthy**.

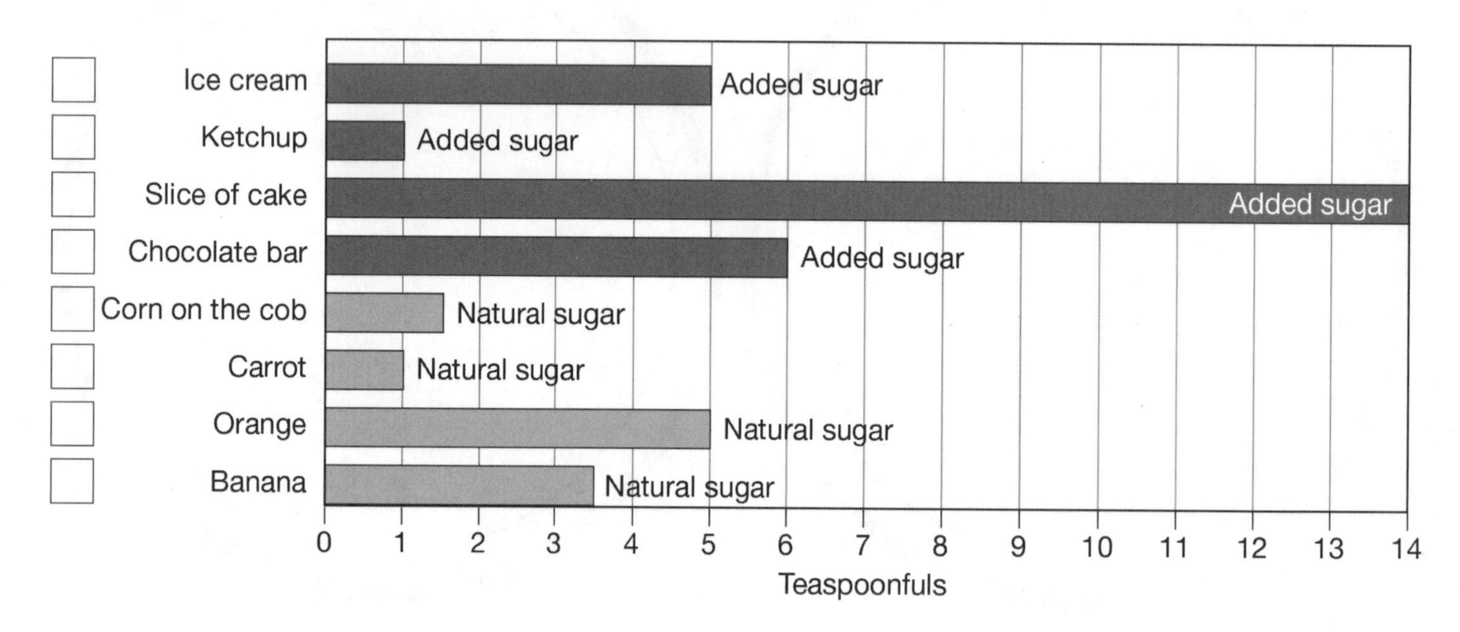

1 **Label each food in the boxes above as H (healthy food) or T (treat).**

2

Think about it!

Sabera eats ice cream ten times a week. Explain why Sabera should eat less ice cream.

___

___

CHECK YOUR LEARNING

- ◯ I know some foods have added sugar.
- ◯ I know that eating foods with lots of added sugar is unhealthy.

2.3 An unhealthy diet

plaque, teeth, heart, kidneys, brain, added salt, muscles, nerves

LOOK AND LEARN

350 ml of cola = 10 teaspoons of white sugar.
So, five drinks of cola a week means 5 x 10 = 50 teaspoons.
250 drinks of cola a year means 250 x 10 = 2500 teaspoons.

KEY FACTS

Added sugar is food for **plaque**, which makes acid that can rot and destroy your **teeth**!

Drinks that harm your teeth

Resources
You will need a calculator.

1 Complete the table on the next page to show the number of teaspoons of sugar you might drink.

Drink	How many teaspoons in 350 ml?	Five drinks a week means...	250 drinks a year means...
orange juice	7 teaspoons	35 teaspoons	1750 teaspoons
water	0 teaspoons	______ teaspoons	______ teaspoons
milk	3 teaspoons	______ teaspoons	______ teaspoons
orange soda	13 teaspoons	______ teaspoons	______ teaspoons
lemonade	6 teaspoons	______ teaspoons	______ teaspoons

2 Which drink would be best for your teeth? ______________________

3 **Think about it!**

What could make cola a safer drink for teeth?

____

____

Salt is good and bad!

KEY FACTS

Our bodies need salt to stay healthy, but eating too much salt can be bad for your blood, your **heart**, your **kidneys** and your **brain**.

There is some salt in all foods, but many foods – such as fried chicken, cereal, tinned foods and butter – contain added salt. Some people also add salt when they are cooking or eating food.

Remember:

It's best to only have about ½–1 teaspoonful of salt each day.

What would you say to the girl eating chips?

____

____

Too much salt is bad for parts of your body

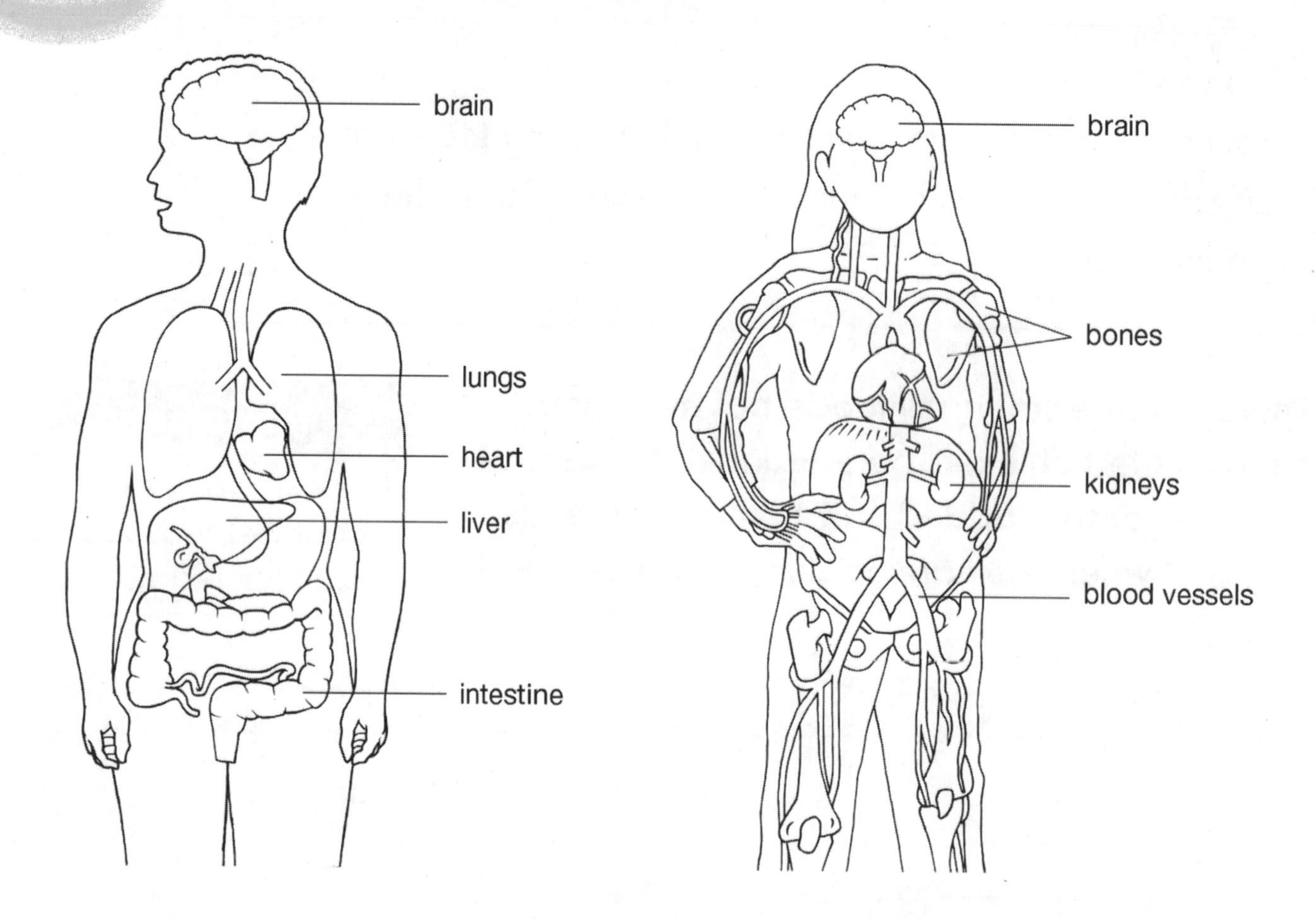

1 Colour in the parts of your body that can be harmed by salt.

2 Name some foods that have added salt.

____

____

3 **Think about it!**

What can you do to eat less added salt?

____

____

Collecting evidence

Read this information about different foods.

Tinned beans

Food group	*per 100 g*
Fat	less than ½ g
Carbohydrate	12 g
Protein	5 g
Salt	½ g

Tinned fish

Food group	*per 100 g*
Fat	27 g
Carbohydrate	almost none
Protein	13 g
Salt	1 g

Rice

Food group	*per 100 g*
Fat	3 g
Carbohydrate	28 g
Protein	3 g
Salt	almost none

1 **If you ate a meal with 100 g of each food above:**

a **How many grams (g) of salt would you eat?** ______________

b **How many grams (g) of carbohydrate would you eat?**

____

c **How many grams (g) of fat would you eat?** ______________

2 **Which food above has the most carbohydrate?** __________

3 **Which food above has the least protein?** ______________

CHECK YOUR LEARNING

- ◯ I know that some foods have added salt.
- ◯ I can say why salt can be unhealthy.
- ◯ I can gather information.
- ◯ I know that too much sugar is bad for my teeth.

2.4 Exercise and sleep

breathe, predict, exercise, results, oxygen

Measuring time

Resources
You will need a stopwatch.

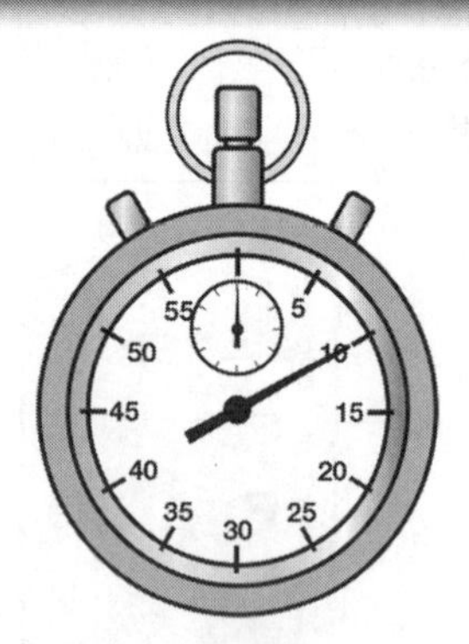

1. Practise measuring 10 seconds on the stopwatch.
2. Try again and see how many times you can write your name in 10 seconds.
3. Now count other things you can do in 10 seconds.

   In 10 seconds I can draw a Sun ________ times.

   In 10 seconds I can ____________________ times.

   In 10 seconds I can ____________________ times.

Testing your heart and lungs

Resources
You will need a clock or watch, and a skipping rope.

1. Put both hands on your chest and **breathe** in and out gently. Can you feel your chest rise and fall? How many breaths in one minute? That is your resting breathing rate.
2. **Predict** which activities in the table on the next page will make your breathing faster, slower or the same.
3. Now do each activity gently for one minute. Then stop and count your breaths for one minute.

   Was your breathing faster, slow or the same?

KEY FACTS

Exercise is good for your heart, bones, nerves and muscles. It makes you feel good and keeps you fit!

	Running on the spot	Sitting	Star jumps
Number of breaths per minute at rest (before the activity)			
Prediction **After the activity, will your breathing be faster, slower or the same?**			
Result **Number of breaths per minute after the test**			
Was your breathing faster, slower or the same?			

4 Look at the **results.** What do you notice?

___

5 Explain why you think this happens.

___

6 **Think about it!**

What kinds of exercise do you do?

___

KEY FACTS

When you exercise, your heart beats faster to get more **oxygen** from your lungs to your muscles so that they can work harder.

CHECK YOUR LEARNING

- ◯ I can use a timer to measure time in seconds.
- ◯ I can explain why exercise is good for my body.

3 Living things

The unit challenge

The activities in this Challenge unit will extend learners' knowledge of the following topics in the Learner's Book and Activity Book:

Topic	In this topic, learners will:
3.1 Living and non-living things	learn about the seven needs of living things
3.2 Growth and nutrition	learn about the growth of different animals
3.3 Movement and reproduction	learn that animals and plants move in different ways and investigate the way seeds can travel from the plant that makes them
3.4 Sorting humans	see that people are similar in some ways but different in others, and that we can use this to sort them
3.5 Sorting living things	sort living things into groups

Help your learner

In this unit, learners will make and record observations (Sections 3.1 and 3.3), make predictions (Section 3.3), present results (Sections 3.3 and 3.4), draw conclusions and begin to use scientific knowledge to suggest explanations (Sections 3.2 and 3.3). To help them:

1 Give learners opportunities to record and present information. Encourage them to draw conclusions: 'What was the result?' 'Why did ... happen?'

TEACHING TIP

Take care with words like 'food' and 'energy'. Humans eat food to get energy; the body uses that energy to function and to move and be active.

3.1 Living and non-living

living, life processes, non-living, hibernate

LOOK AND LEARN

We know if something is **living** because it carries out the seven **life processes** of breathing, needing water and food, moving, having senses, being able to produce young, growing, and producing waste products.

Seven life processes

Use what you know and can find out to fill in the last two columns in the table.

	Tuna	Eagle	Goat
The way it breathes	through gills		
Does it eat?	yes		
The way it moves	swims		
Does it lay eggs or produce live young?	lays eggs		
Does it produce waste?	yes		

Remember:

Tables like the one above are a way that scientists present information.

KEY FACTS

Which group of animals has the most numbers alive today? The insects! There are 7 billion humans and perhaps around 2 trillion insects!

Doubting Dana

1 **Dana often gets her science wrong. Read her comments and explain why she is wrong.**

2 **Think about it!**

Some animals hibernate in cold weather – they go into a deep, deep sleep. Are they living or are they non-living?

____

____

CHECK YOUR LEARNING

○ I can talk about the seven life processes.

3.2 Growth and nutrition

life cycle, adult

Life cycles

Use the words in the boxes below to make the life cycle for each animal.

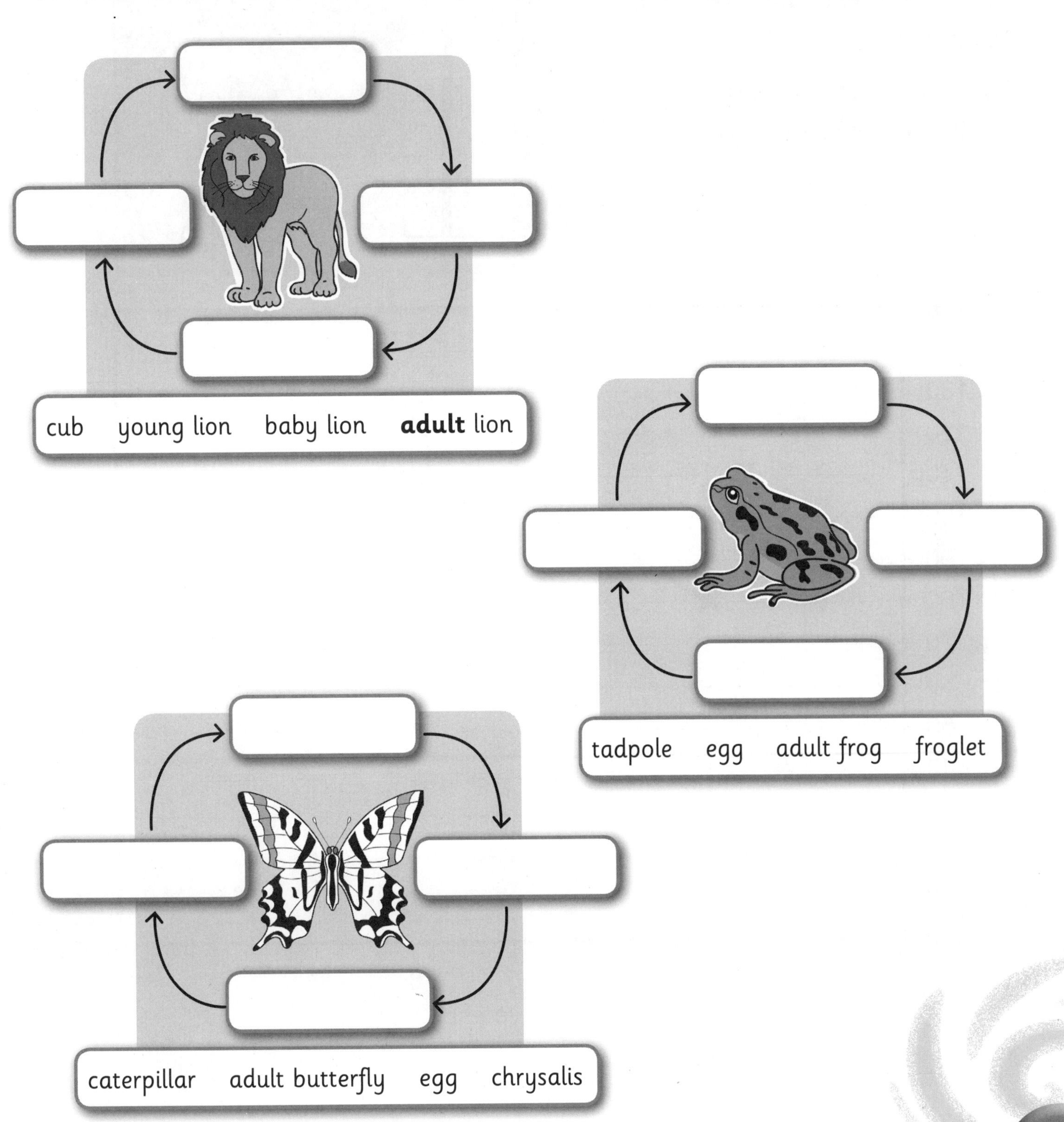

Chet's growth graph

Chet's family have marked his growth on this post outside his house. Chet has a ruler so that you can now draw a graph of his growth.

1 Plot this information onto the line graph below.

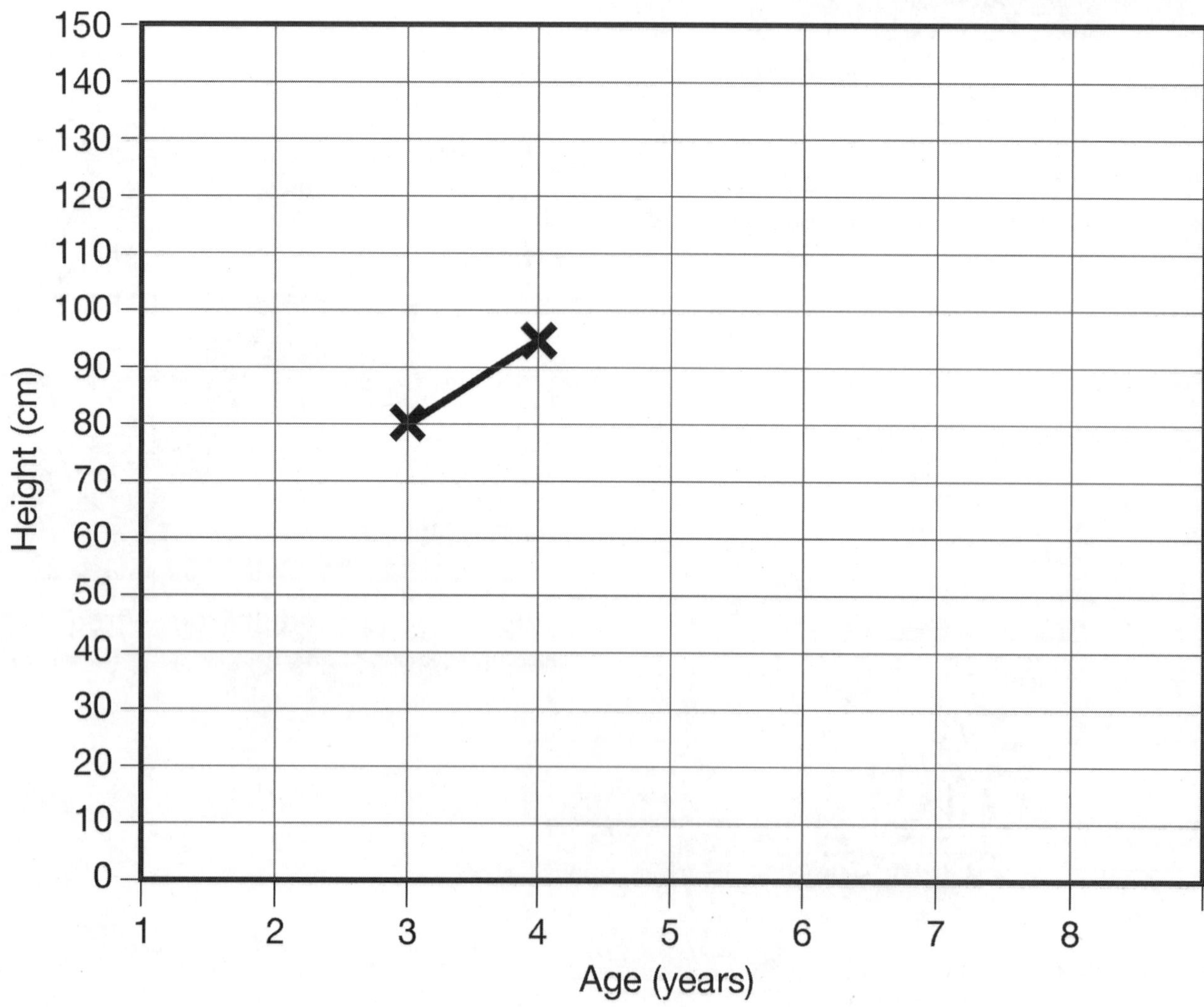

2 What was Chet's height at four years old? __________cm

3 How many centimetres did Chet grow between his third and sixth birthdays? __________cm

4 What was Chet's height at five and a half years? __________cm

5 How many centimetres tall might Chet be on his eighth birthday?
__________cm

KEY FACTS

Humans will only grow normally if they eat a balanced, healthy diet and take exercise.

6 **Think about it!**

Imagine that we found another planet like Earth and moved to live there. Astronauts could not take all the food they needed. What could they do to have enough food to stay on the new planet?

____

____

CHECK YOUR LEARNING

- ◯ I know that all healthy living things grow until they are an adult.
- ◯ I know that all living things need food.

3.3 Movement and reproduction

question, record

KEY FACTS

Animals move in lots of different ways, for example running, jumping, slithering, crawling, swimming and flying. Plants usually move more slowly: they turn to face the Sun, they spread their roots to make more shoots and their seeds can travel.

Travelling seeds

Seeds can travel from the plant that makes them by falling and bouncing on the ground, floating on water or the wind, and in other ways too.

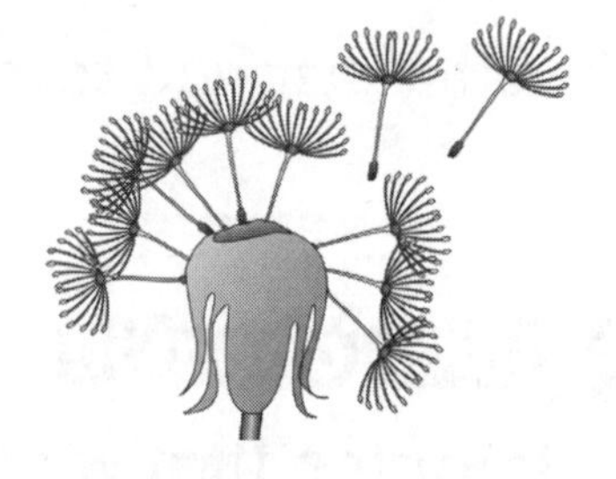

Resources

You will need seeds or small plastic bricks, a tape measure or ruler, paper, chalk and a pencil.

Look at the test the children carried out. Their question is:

How many centimetres do seeds bounce when they drop from a seed pod?

The plastic bricks bounce in a similar way to seeds.

1 Carry this test out from a height you choose and **record** your results. Decide how many times you will test the seeds/bricks. 12 times? 15 times? 20 times? Predict what you think the results may be. Make a table here to record your results.

2 What was the longest bounce? ___________

3 What was the shortest bounce? ___________

4 If there was a score in the middle, what was it? ___________

5 It was a good idea to test many bricks or seeds. Why is this a good idea?

____

____

Remember:

Scientists often repeat a test so that they can trust the answer they get.

CHECK YOUR LEARNING

◯ I know that all living things move in lots of different ways.

3.4 Sorting humans

fingerprint, sort, different, similar, observe, Carroll diagram

We can use features such as **fingerprint** pattern or hair colour to **sort** people into groups.

KEY FACTS

Fingerprints are all **different** so the police use them to identify people. In one million people you might not even find one person with **similar** fingerprints to you!

Patterns in fingerprints!

Resources
You might find a magnifying glass helpful.

1 **Observe** different peoples' fingerprints and record them below. Try to examine the fingers of at least six different people of any age.

Loop	Arch	Whorl

2 Which pattern was most common in your group of people? ______________________

3 Which pattern was least common in your group?

____

Grouping people

Look at this table.

Name	Boy or girl?	Age	Fingerprint pattern	Handed
Julio	Boy	9	Loop	Right-handed
Isabella	Girl	9	Whorl	Right-handed
Qiao	Boy	8	Loop	Right-handed
Luciana	Girl	9	Arch	Right-handed
Waheed	Boy	9	Whorl	Left-handed
Amira	Girl	8	Arch	Right-handed

1 Complete this **Carroll diagram** to group the children.

	Boy	Girl
8 years old		
9 years old	Julio	Isabella

2 Make your own Carroll diagram based on handedness and fingerprint pattern.

CHECK YOUR LEARNING

○ I can group people in different ways.

invertebrate

Sorting invertebrates

Look at these invertebrates.

KEY FACTS

Scientists divide the animal kingdom into two big groups – animals with backbones (such as humans) and animals without backbones (invertebrates).

This pie chart shows there are many more invertebrates.

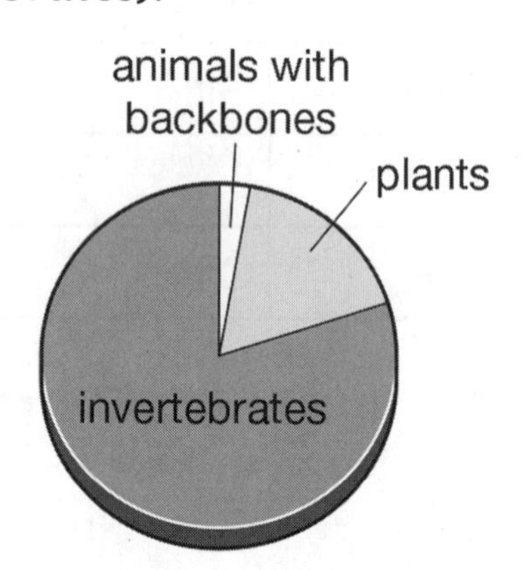

There are many ways to sort them by asking questions, for example: *Does the animal live on land?*

1. **Think of other questions you could ask to sort the invertebrates.**
2. **Choose two of your questions and sort the invertebrates. Do any fit into both groups?**

CHECK YOUR LEARNING

- ◯ I can observe that living things have something in common.
- ◯ I can sort living things into groups.

4 Our five senses

The unit challenge

The activities in this Challenge unit will extend learners' knowledge of the following topics in the Learner's Book and Activity Book:

Topic	In this topic, learners will:
4.1 Hearing and touch	recognise things we hear with our ears and touch with our skin
4.2 Taste and smell	understand that we taste with our tongue and smell with our nose
4.3 Sight	investigate if our eyes can see to the side

Help your learner

In this unit, learners will observe and compare objects (Section 4.1), make predictions (Section 4.2), collect evidence (Sections 4.1 and 4.2) and record observations (Sections 4.1 and 4.3). They will also present results, draw conclusions and begin to use scientific knowledge to suggest explanations (Sections 4.2 and 4.3). To help them:

1 Help learners explore the sense of taste by encouraging them to try different foods. Use the opportunity to talk about eating healthy foods and avoiding less healthy foods.

Stress safety when talking about the senses. For example, remind learners to never look directly at the Sun and avoid loud sounds.

TEACHING TIP

When you talk with learners about taste, try to refer to bitter and sour tastes as well as sweet. They may not be so familiar, but they are important in science.

4.1 Hearing and touch

hearing, touch, smell, taste, sight, vibrates, vocal cords

Quiet or loud?

1 Look at the pictures and label them as very quiet, quiet, loud or very loud.

KEY FACTS

Our five senses are **hearing**, **touch**, **smell**, **taste** and **sight**. You use your two ears to hear things and your skin to touch.

Very loud sounds can damage your ears. Avoid very loud sounds.

2 Think about it!

Sounds are made when material **vibrates** in air. Rest one hand on the front of your neck and count to ten. Your **vocal cords** are moving. Can you describe the way they feel when they move?

____

Hear it and touch it

Look around the room or building, or go outside if it is safe.
Find things you can hear or touch. Describe what they feel or sound like.

What is it?	Can we hear it or touch it?	What does it feel or sound like?
a plane	hear it	very loud, like a motorbike

KEY FACTS

Your skin can feel things that are hot, cold, wet, dry, rough and smooth. Your sense of touch means that you can name objects and materials with your eyes shut.

CHECK YOUR LEARNING

- ◯ I know about my five senses.
- ◯ I know that I use my ears to hear and my skin to touch.

bar chart, tongue, fair test

Favourite salad foods

1 Look at these salad foods. Draw and label another salad food of your own choice.

2 Ask eight people which of these salad foods is their favourite. Note the answers and put the results on a **bar chart**.

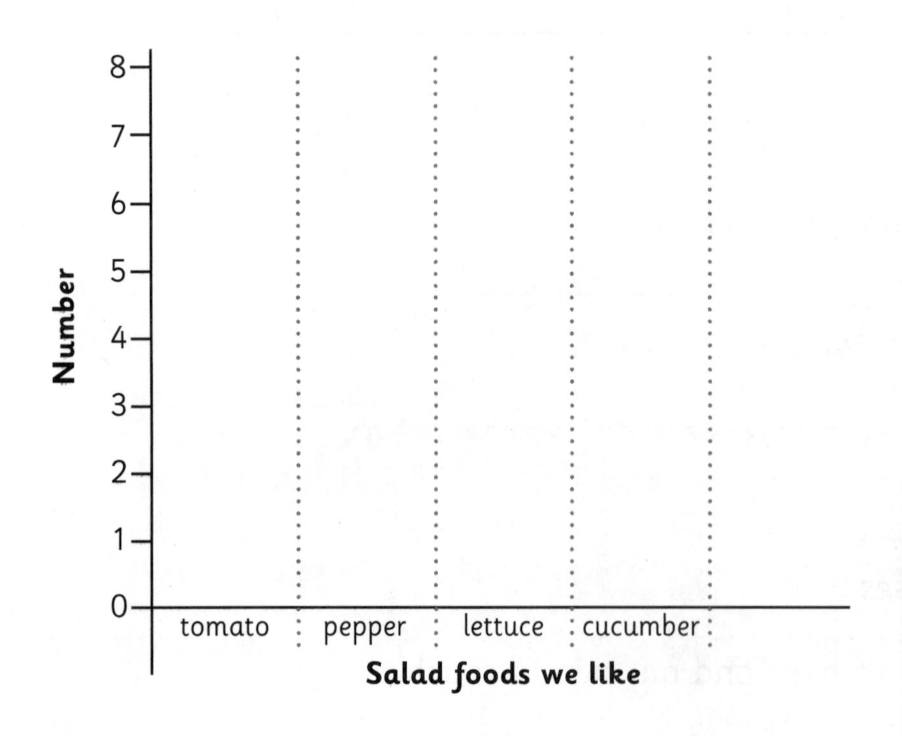

3 Which salad food was the most popular?

____

4 Which salad food was the second most popular?

____

KEY FACTS

You use your **tongue** to taste and your nose to smell.

Can you smell the sweet?

Resources
You will need fruit-flavoured sweets (unwrapped), a blindfold and a ruler.

Put a sweet on the table. Move close enough so you can smell it. Would you know what flavour it is just from the smell?

You are going to find out from what distance a person can still smell a sweet and tell you the flavour of the sweet correctly.

Think: How many people will I test? What will I do to make it a **fair test**?

1 **Write what you will do in four steps.**

1. First I will…	2. Then I will…	3. Then I will…	4. Then I will…

2 **Before you start, predict what you think will happen.**

____

3 **Carry out your test. Then make a table here to record your results.**

4 **Which flavour could people smell from the greatest distance?** __________

CHECK YOUR LEARNING

◯ I know that I taste with my tongue and smell with my nose.

investigation

Can we see to the side?

Resources
You will need three people to help you, an object to hold and pens.

Look at the picture.
Atif faces forward and does not turn his head. Riya holds an object at different points and asks if Atif can see it. After the test, Riya records the result like this.

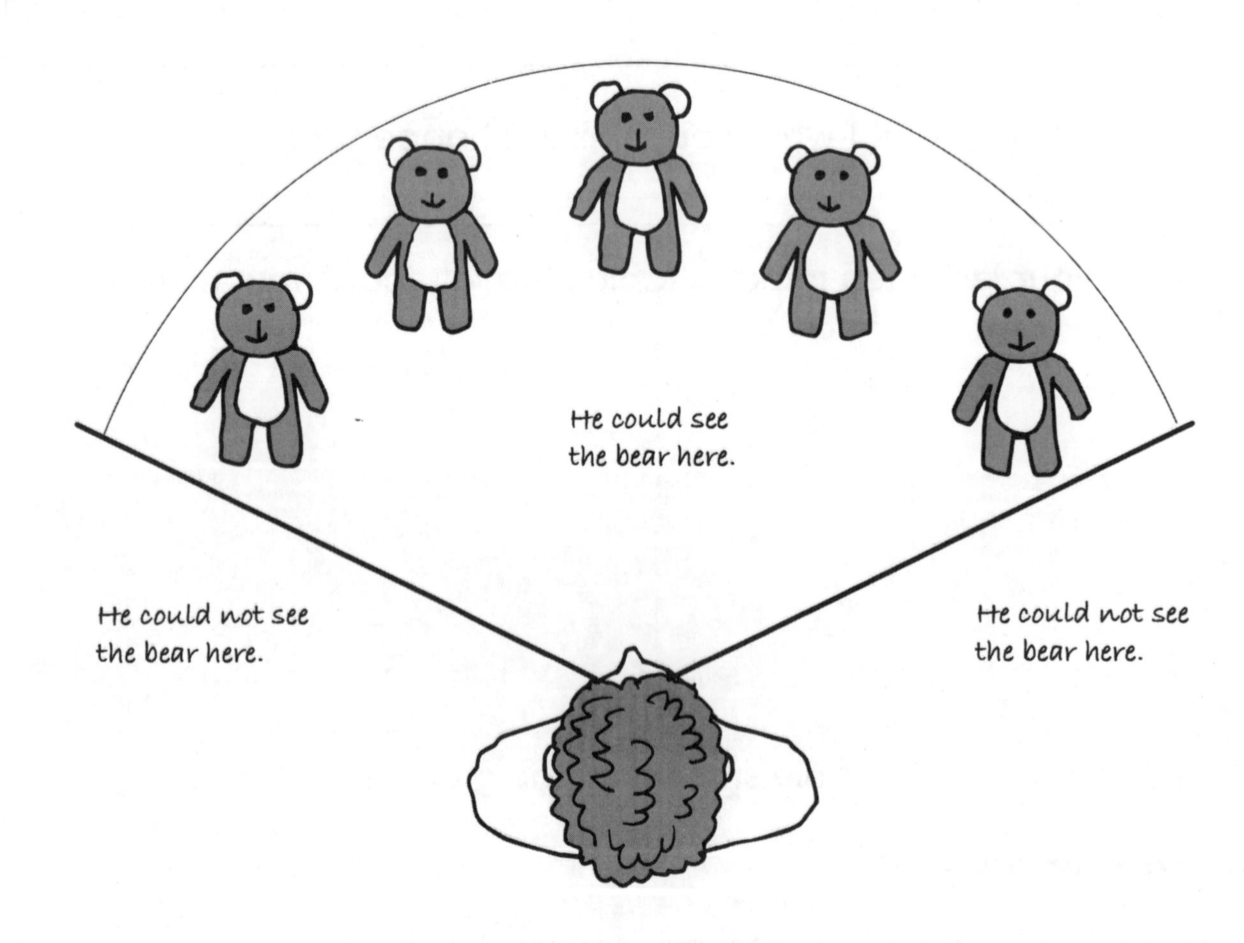

1 Now carry out your own **investigation** with three different people. Record the results below. (Use a different colour for each person.)

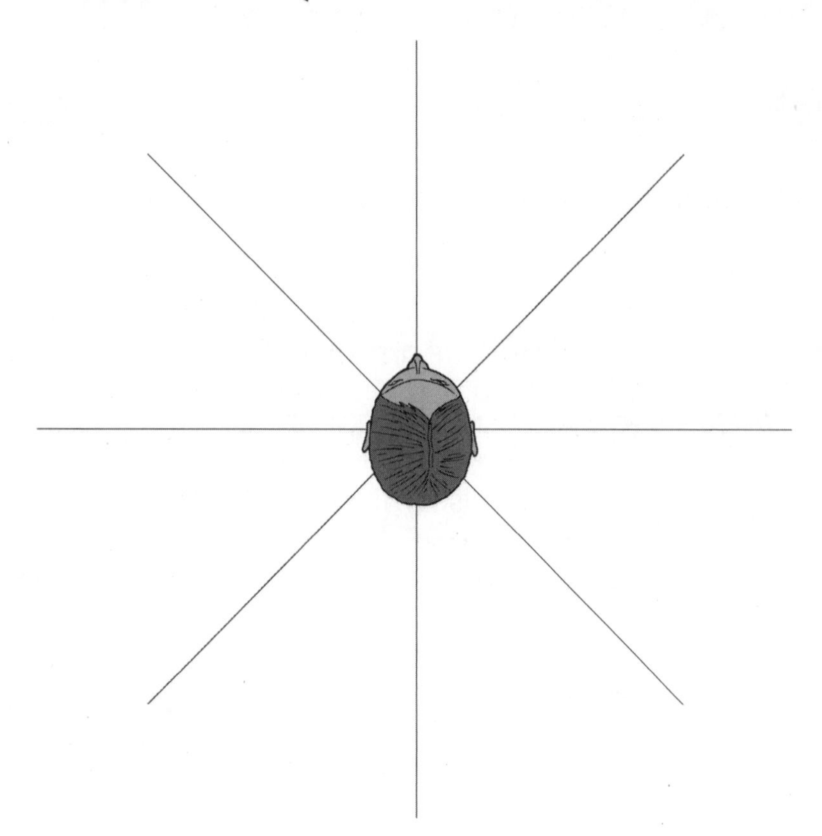

2 Humans can see forwards. But can we see to the side?

____

3 **Think about it!**

Human babies have quite poor eyesight. Why do you think a baby does not need good eyesight?

____

CHECK YOUR LEARNING

- ◯ I know that I should care for my eyes.
- ◯ I know that I cannot see all the way around my head.

> **!** Take care of your eyes. Keep them clean and never look directly at the Sun or other very bright lights.

5 Investigating materials

The unit challenge

The activities in this Challenge unit will extend learners' knowledge of the following topics in the Learner's Book and Activity Book:

Topic	In this topic, learners will:
5.1 Properties of materials	see Skills Builder, Section 5.1
5.2 Sorting materials	sort materials by their properties
5.3 Uses of materials	draw conclusions from the results of experiments
5.4 Testing materials	investigate the strength of different types of paper
5.5 Magnetic materials	see Skills Builder, Section 5.5

Help your learner

In this unit, learners will practise observing and comparing objects (Section 5.2). They will also present results in drawings, bar charts and tables (Section 5.4), draw conclusions from results and begin to identify simple patterns (Sections 5.3 and 5.4). To help them:

1 In Section 5.2, learners will benefit from repeating sorting activities using different criteria. Ask learners to sort objects by size, colour or by how absorbent they are.

2 In Section 5.4, help learners to check that their test is fair by using the same coin and dropping it the same way each time.

TEACHING TIP

When we measure in grams and kilos we measure the mass of an object. Try to use this word. In daily life we use the word 'weight', but this is incorrect. Weight is correctly measured in newtons.

5.2 Sorting materials

rough, smooth, rigid, flexible, property, Venn diagram, hard, absorbent, strong, soft

Line up

Materials can be sorted into groups but they can also be put in order.

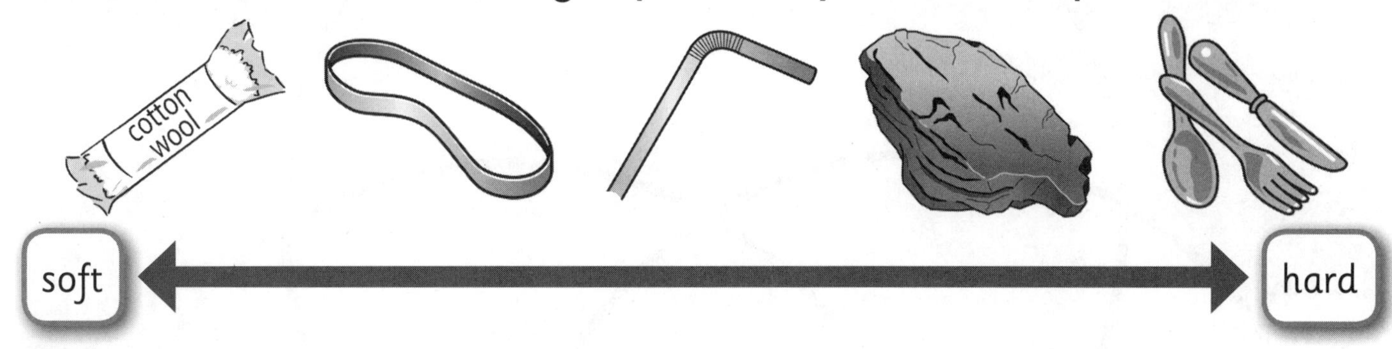

1 Find some materials and put them in order from **rough** to **smooth**.

2 Now order them from **rigid** to **flexible**.

3 Now order them using another **property**. You could use colour or strength.

Venn diagram

1 Choose some materials and sort them into the empty **Venn diagram** on the next page.

LOOK AND LEARN

Venn diagrams with three circles can be used to sort materials.

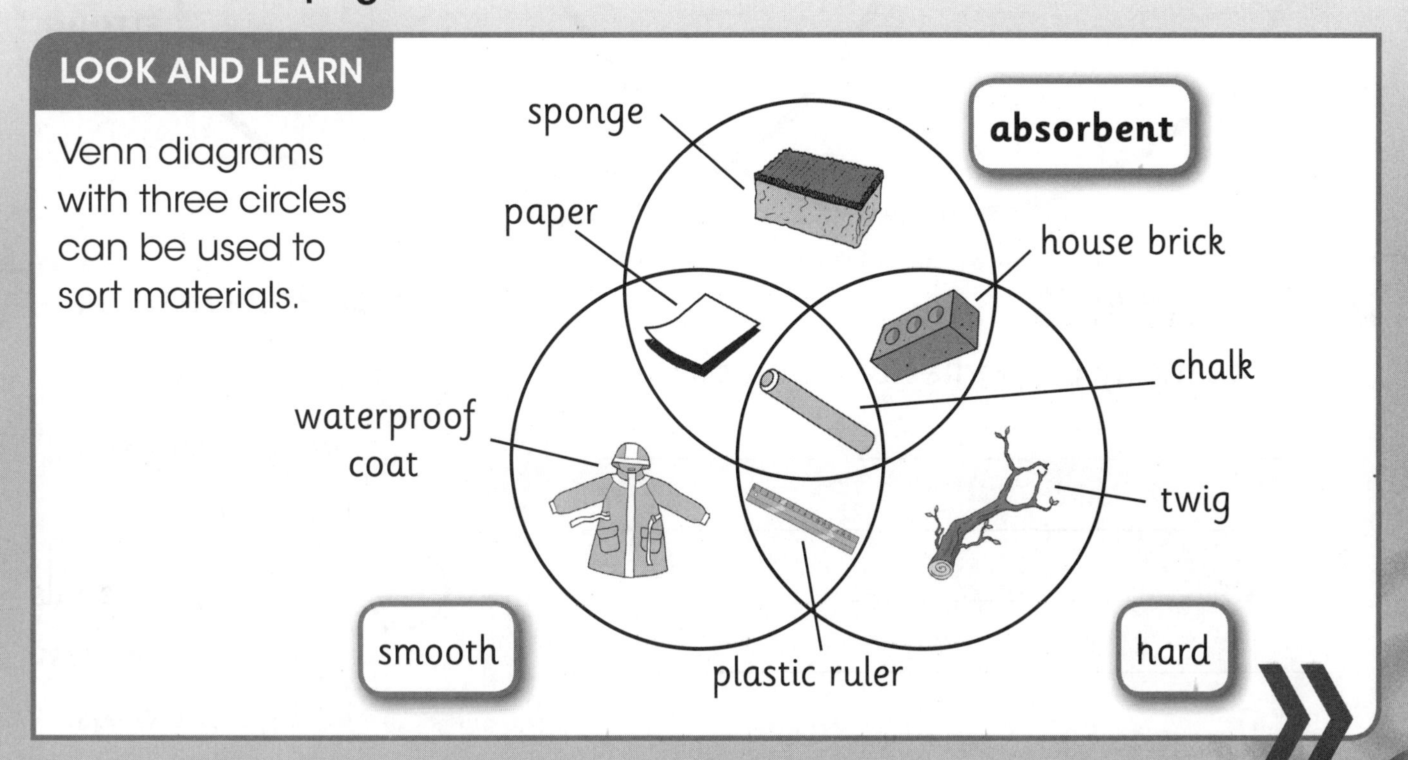

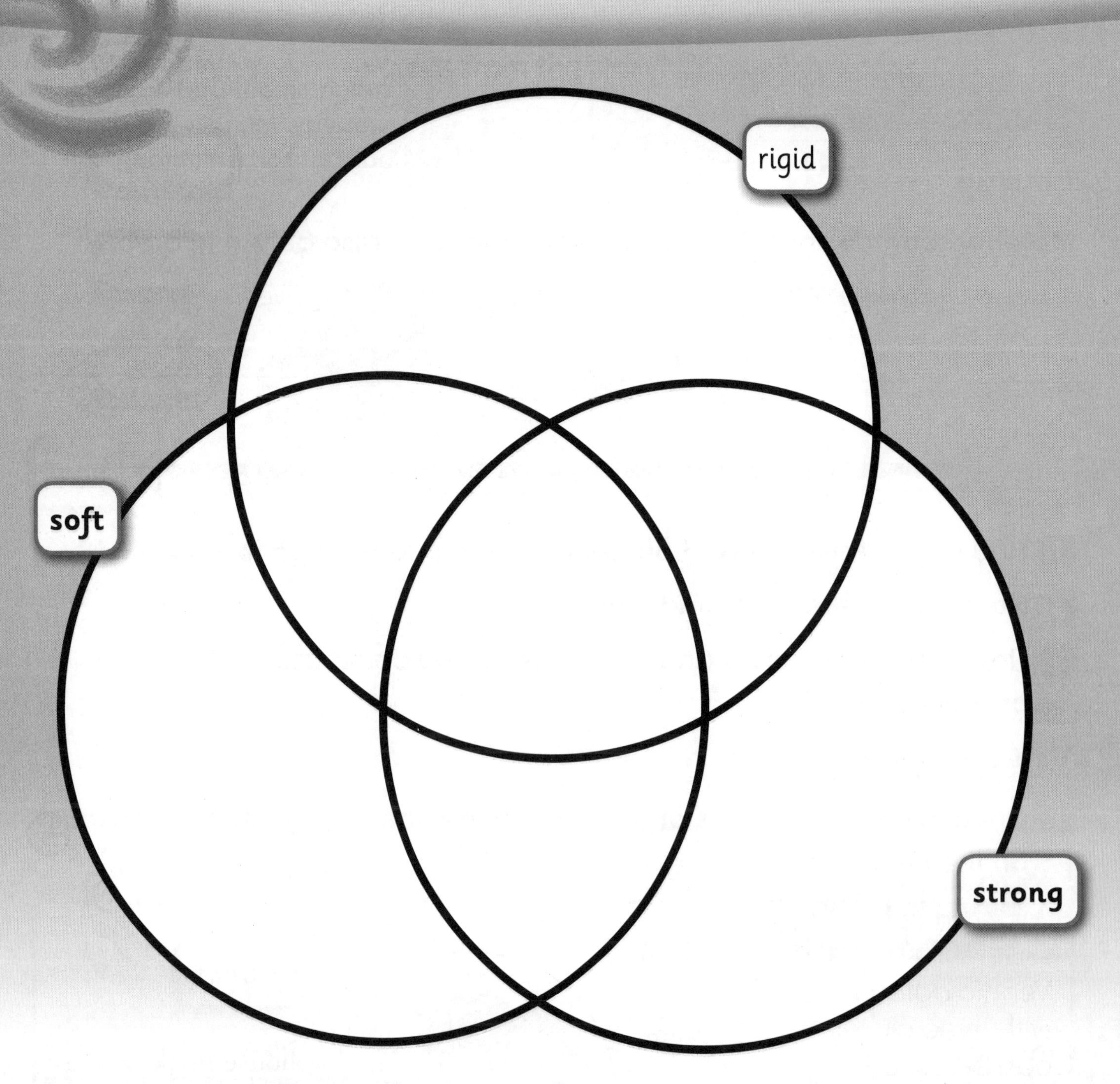

2 Think about it!

List as many properties of metal as you can.

____

____

____

____

CHECK YOUR LEARNING

- ◯ I can name the properties of some materials.
- ◯ I can sort materials by their properties in different ways.

5.3 Uses of materials

bridge, mass

The strongest bridge

Akshay's class are making model **bridges**. Some children have used plastic, some have used paper straws and some have used wood. They are testing the strength of each bridge.

They have tested six bridges. Here are their results.

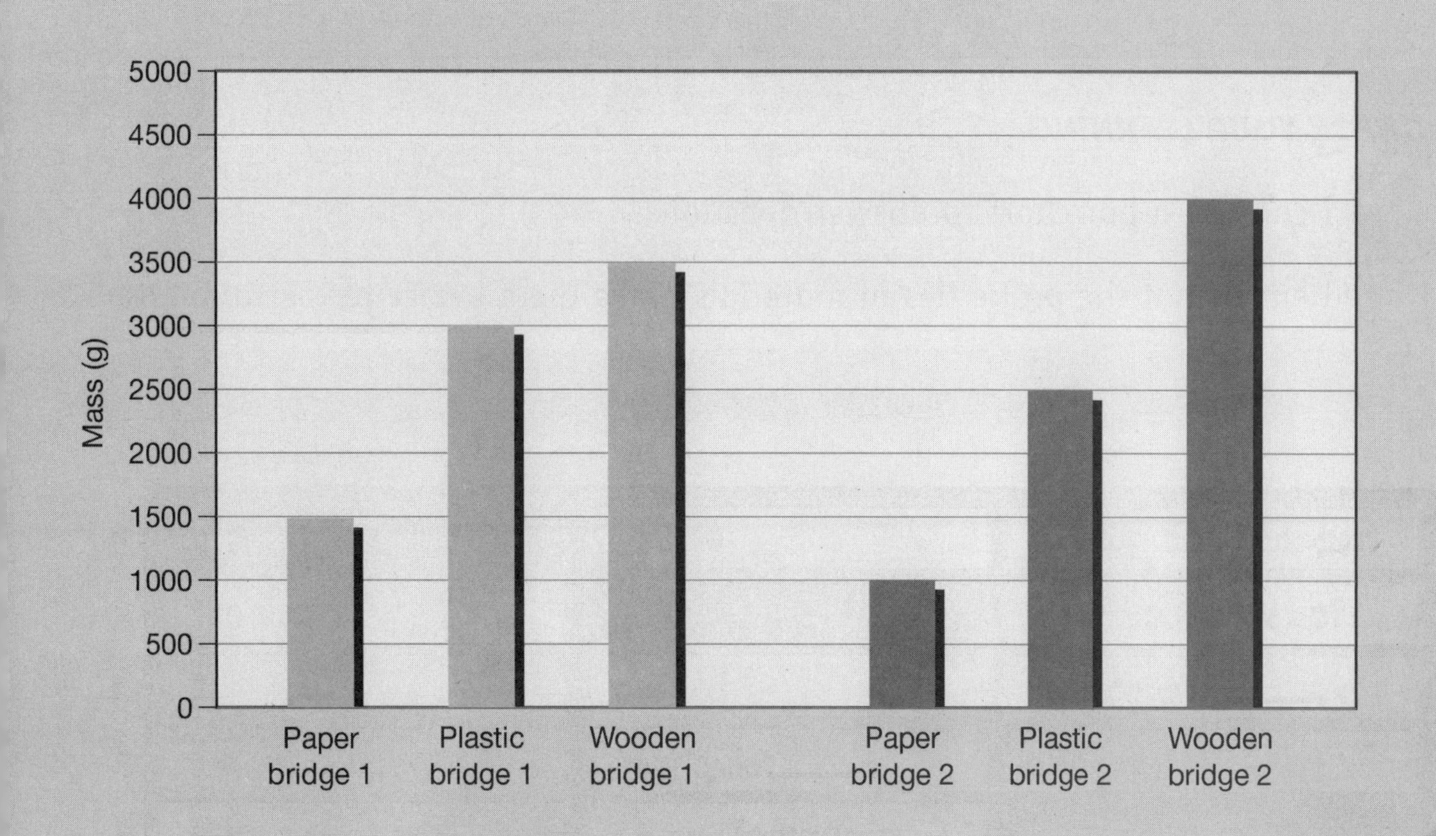

1 How many grams (g) of **mass** did plastic bridge 1 hold?

____

2 How many grams (g) did wooden bridge 1 hold?

____

3 Which bridge was the strongest?

____

4 Which bridge was the weakest?

____

5 Which of these materials is the best for a strong model bridge?

____

6 **Think about it!**

What other strong materials are used to make real bridges?

____

CHECK YOUR LEARNING

- ◯ I can use a bar chart to answer questions.
- ◯ I know that the properties of materials make them better for certain jobs.

5.4 Testing materials

Which paper is strongest when wet?

Resources
You will need a container of water, a ruler, a coin, three plastic cups, some writing paper, a paper towel and some toilet paper.

1. Put each piece of paper in water then over the top of a plastic cup.
2. Look at the picture to see what to do next.
3. Drop the coin from higher up each time until the paper tears.
4. Write your result in the table.
5. Now test the other pieces of paper.

	Writing paper	Paper towel	Toilet paper
Height of coin when paper tears			

Draw a bar chart

Remember:

Use a ruler to draw neat bars.

1 Use your results from the test to draw a bar chart in the grid below.

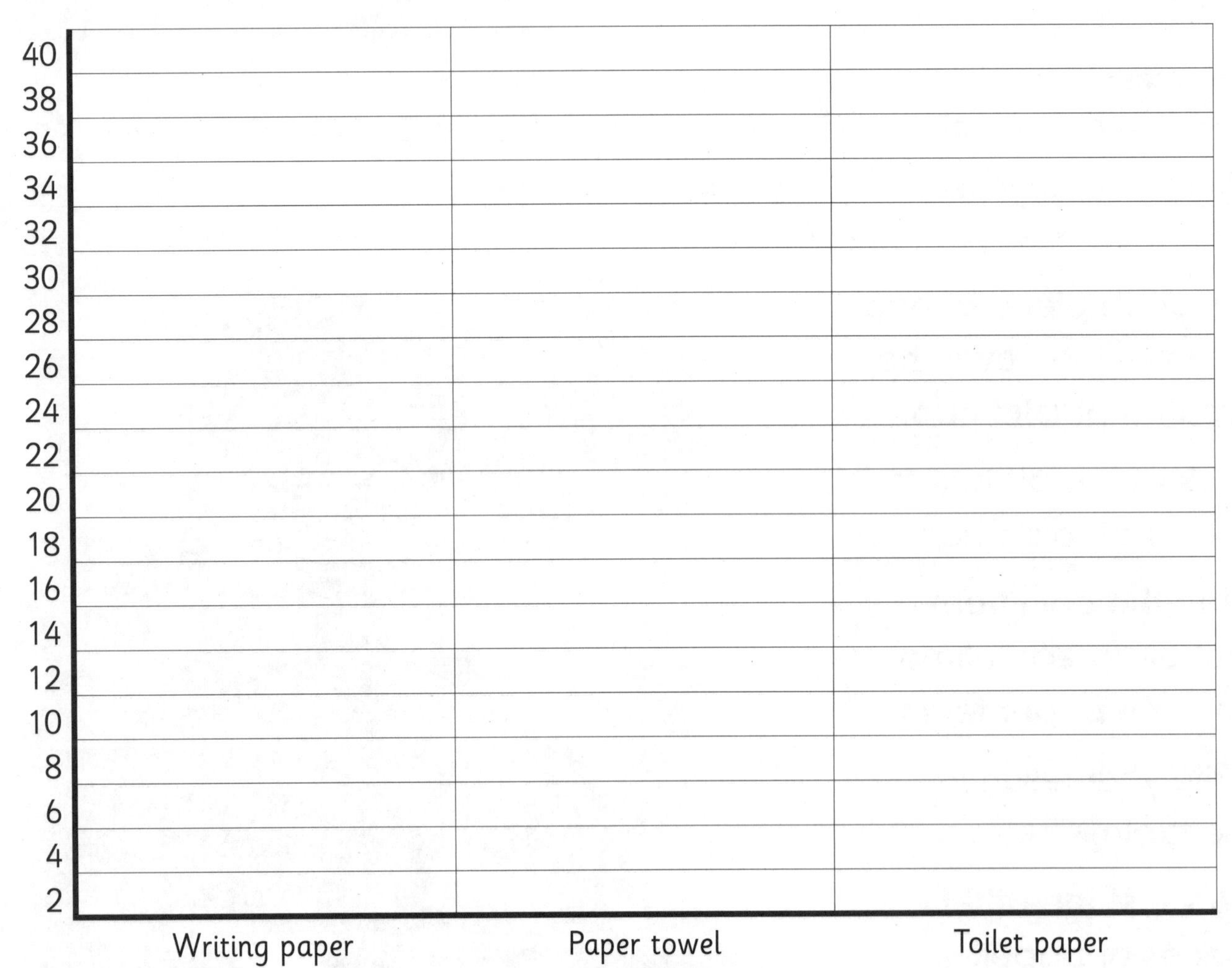

2 Which paper was the strongest when wet? ____________________

3 Which paper was the weakest when wet? ____________________

4 **Think about it!**

Why does a paper towel need to be strong when it is wet?

____

____

CHECK YOUR LEARNING

◯ I can measure carefully.

◯ I can show my results in a bar chart.

6 Forces and movement

The unit challenge

The activities in this Challenge unit will extend learners' knowledge of the following topics in the Learner's Book and Activity Book:

Topic	In this topic, learners will:
6.1 Push and pull	learn that a push and pull together can make a twisting or turning force
6.2 Changing shape	see Skills Builder, Section 6.2
6.3 How big is that force?	compare the weight of different objects and see that forces can make things change direction
6.4 Forcemeters	see Skills Builder, Section 6.4
6.5 Friction	compare the friction of different surfaces

Help your learner

In this unit, learners will practise collecting evidence to answer questions or test ideas (Sections 6.3 and 6.5), observing and comparing objects, living things and events (Sections 6.1, 6.3 and 6.5) and measuring using simple equipment and recording observations (Sections 6.3 and 6.5). They will also present results, draw conclusions from results and begin to use scientific knowledge to suggest explanations (Sections 6.3 and 6.5). To help them:

TEACHING TIP

Help learners to measure carefully by asking them to check each measurement to make sure it is correct.

1 Discuss with them how to make enquiries fair by only changing one thing each time. In Section 6.3, they should use the same rubber band each time and only change the object. In Section 6.5, they should use the same coin and the same force each time and only change the surface.

6.1 Push and pull

twist, turn, force, push, pull

LOOK AND LEARN

A **twisting** or **turning force** is made when you **push** on one side of an object and **pull** on the other side. For example, to take the top off a bottle, you push on one side of the top and pull on the other.

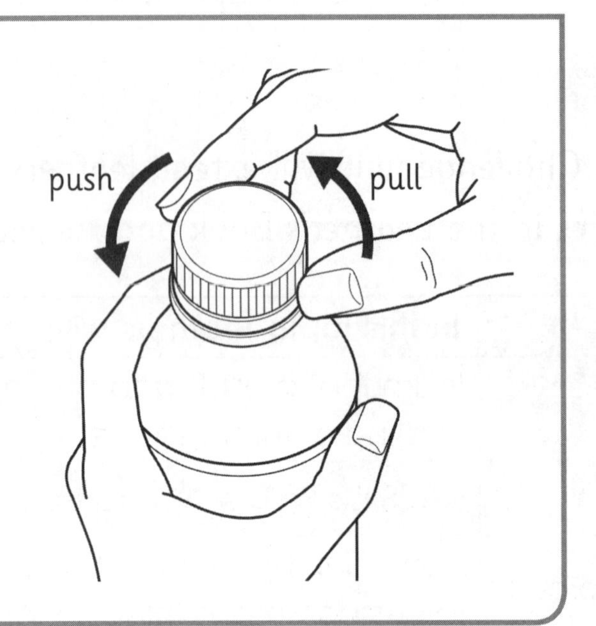

Do the twist

1. Find some objects that you can twist or turn.
2. Draw and label the objects.
3. **Think about it!**
   A twist or turn is a push and a pull together. Will a bottle top turn if you push on both sides?

   ____

CHECK YOUR LEARNING

○ I know that a push and pull together can make a twisting or turning force.

6.3 How big is that force?

forcemeter, gravity, weight

Comparing weight

Resources
You will need a 30 cm ruler, a rubber band and a paper clip.

KEY FACTS

Gravity causes **weight** because it pulls objects towards the ground.

1. Make a simple **forcemeter**. Put the rubber band over the zero end of the ruler. Put your finger on the end of the ruler to hold the rubber band.
2. Bend the paper clip into a hook and put it onto the rubber band.
3. Now put different objects onto the hook to see the length the rubber band stretches.
4. Write each object and the length of the rubber band in the table. Start by writing the length of the rubber band with no object on the hook.

Object	Length of rubber band
No object	

Be safe! Do not use objects that might break. Do not use heavy objects that will break the rubber band.

Remember:

Only measure the length of the rubber band each time.

5 **Finish these sentences by writing about the weight of the objects.**

a When the rubber band is short, the weight is ______________________.

b When the rubber band is long, the weight is ______________________.

c The longer the rubber band, the ______________________________.

LOOK AND LEARN

A bungee jumper uses a very larger rubber band called a bungee. The force from the bungee stops the person falling down and makes them go back up. Forces can make things change direction.

6 **Think about it!**

Why do bungee jumpers have to know the length the bungee will stretch to?

____

7 **When you throw a ball up in the air, what force makes it change direction and fall back down?** ________________

CHECK YOUR LEARNING

- ◯ I can compare the size of different forces.
- ◯ I know that forces can make things change direction.

6.5 Friction

slide, surface, friction

Resources
You will need a coin and a tape measure or long ruler.

Sliding coins

When you **slide** a coin on a **surface**, there is **friction** between the coin and the surface. The less friction there is, the further the coin will slide.

Remember:
Try to push the coin with the same force each time.

1. Slide a coin on different surfaces.
2. Measure how many centimetres the coin went on each surface and fill in the table.

Surface	Distance the coin went (cm)

3. Which surface had the most friction? ______________________
4. Which surface had the least friction? ______________________
5. **Think about it!**
   What would happen if a surface had no friction?

   ____

   ____

CHECK YOUR LEARNING

○ I can compare the friction of different surfaces.

Answers

1 Looking after plants

1.2

Plant growth

1 Day 1 – 2 cm. Day 10 – 3 cm. Day 20 – 5 cm. Day 30 – 4 cm.

2 2 cm

3 The number of leaves increased.

4 The plant has wilted because it has not been watered.

5 water

6 **Think about it!**
Plants grow taller in the dark because they are trying to grow upwards to find some light. (If a plant was growing from a seed planted very deep in soil, the plant would find light by growing up and out of the soil.)

1.4

The best place for plants

1 The best place is Place 2 because it is not too hot or too cold. Most plants grow best when it is warm.

2 a thermometer

3 Plants that are too hot or too cold might not grow well or they might wilt or they might die.

4 **Think about it!**
Water freezes into ice when it is very cold. If water has frozen into ice, this would make it hard for roots to absorb water.

2 Looking after ourselves

2.1

A balanced diet

1

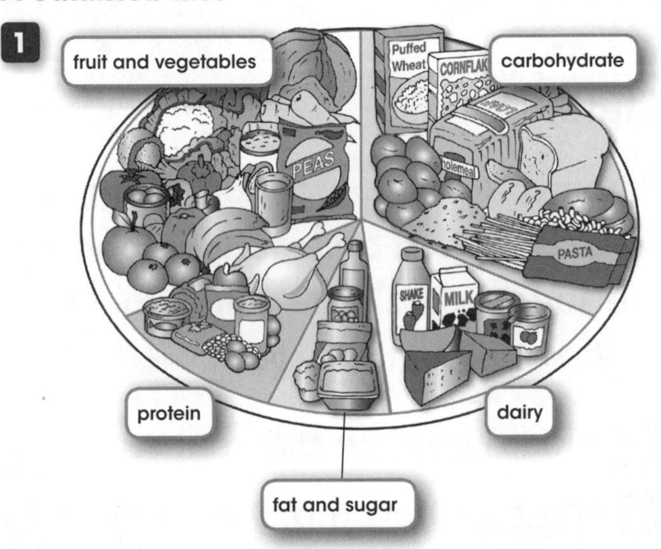

2 and 3 On each plate foods should be drawn which may include the person's preferences (Sima – fruit, sweets and cheese; Sam meat and fruit) and other foods in appropriately balanced proportions.

4 **Think about it!**
Learners give examples of popular foods and suggest that healthy options can be eaten regularly but that unhealthy ones be eaten just occasionally, for example two or three times per week.

2.2

Healthy or treat?

1 Ice cream = T
Ketchup = H
Pastry = T
Chocolate bar = T
Corn on the cob = H
Carrot = H
Orange = H (but high in natural sugar)
Banana – H (but high in natural sugar)

2 **Think about it!**

Ice cream can be full of fat and sugar; the answer can mention this. Learners might also refer to possible tooth decay or a possible increase in weight.

2.3

Drinks that harm your teeth

1

Drink	How many teaspoons in 350 ml?	Five drinks a week means...	250 drinks a year means...
orange juice	7 teaspoons	35 teaspoons	1750 teaspoons
water	0 teaspoons	0 teaspoons	0 teaspoons
milk	3 teaspoons	15 teaspoons	750 teaspoons
orange soda	13 teaspoons	65 teaspoons	3250 teaspoons
lemonade	6 teaspoons	30 teaspoons	1500 teaspoons

2 water

3 **Think about it!**

The learner might suggest less sugar, other ingredients, smaller cans.

Salt is good and bad!

The girl eating chips needs to realise that too much salt is unhealthy.

Too much salt is bad for parts of your body

1 Coloured parts can be brain, heart, blood vessels, kidneys.

2 Any foods to which salt has been added, for example fried chicken or tinned foods.

3 **Think about it!**

The answer should suggest putting less salt on food, not using salt in cooking and/or eating fewer foods that have already had salt added to them (many processed foods).

Collecting evidence

1 **a** 1½ g
b 40 g
c 30 g or 30½ g

2 Rice

3 Rice

2.4

Measuring time

3 The learner gives answers which are reasonable based on their choices.
For example:
In 10 seconds I can draw a Sun 1–3 times.
In 10 seconds I can hop 10 times.

Testing your heart and lungs

1 Accept a breathing rate at rest of around 20–25 breaths per minute.

2 Learners should have recorded their predictions in the table.

3 Results should show exercise leading to increased heart beat and breathing rate.

4 Any reasonable observation is accepted, but ideally that both heart and breathing increase with exercise.

5 This is to help the body get more oxygen.

6 **Think about it!**

Personal answer

3 Living things

3.1

Seven life processes

	Tuna	Eagle	Goat
The way it breathes	through gills	mouth	mouth
Does it eat?	yes	yes	yes
The way it moves	swims	walks and flies	walks and runs
Does it lay eggs or produce live young?	lays eggs	lays eggs	produces live young
Does it produce waste?	yes	yes	yes

Doubting Dana

1. The learner explains that a candle is non-living because it does not breathe, eat, move, have senses, have young, grow or produce waste.

   The learner explains that the snail is living because it breathes, eats, moves, has senses, has young, grows and produces waste.

   The learner explains that the river is non-living because it does not breathe, eat, move, have senses, have young, grow or produce waste.

2. **Think about it!**
   Animals that hibernate are living, just in a very deep sleep.

3.2

Life cycles

1. Lion – baby lion, cub, young lion, adult lion
   Frog – egg, tadpole, froglet, adult frog
   Butterfly – egg, caterpillar, chrysalis, adult butterfly

Chet's growth graph

1.

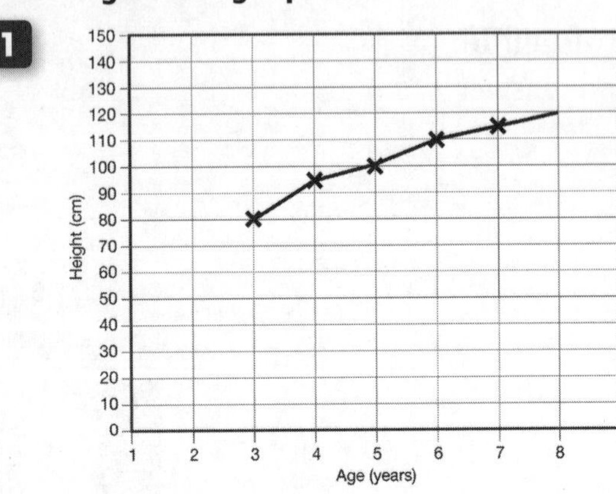

2. 95 cm
3. 30 cm
4. 105 cm
5. Any answer between 120 cm and 125 cm
6. **Think about it!**
   To have enough food on the new planet, astronauts could grow plants and even animals (of course the animals would also need food!).

3.3

Travelling seeds

1. The learner will carry out the test, making a table to record their results.
2. The learner will identify the longest bounce based on their data.
3. The learner will identify the shortest bounce based on their data.
4. The learner will identify a score in the middle of their results.
5. Accept any answer which includes one of these ideas. Repeated tests give more reliablility. It means that you can be sure about your results. Testing once might give you a strange result.

3.4

Patterns in fingerprints!

1. The learner will have recorded their results in the table.
2. The learner will identify the most common pattern based on their data.
3. The learner will identify the least common pattern based on their data.

Grouping people

1. The Carroll diagram should be completed like this:

	Boy	Girl
8 years old	Qiao	Amira
9 years old	Julio, Waheed	Isabella, Luciana

2 The learner should then construct a Carroll diagram similar to this:

	Left-handed	Right-handed
Loop		Julio, Qiao
Whorl	Waheed	Isabella
Arch		Luciana, Amira

3.5

Sorting invertebrates

1 There are many questions that could be asked. For example:
Does the animal eat plants?
Is the animal slimy?
Does it have a shell?
Does it like damp conditions?
Does it have six legs?
Does it live in water?
Can it fly?

2 The learner will have sorted the invertebrates according to their two questions and also identified whether any animals would go into both groups.

4 Our five senses

4.1

Quiet or loud?

1 There is a little flexibility here in the answer you can expect, for example an alarm clock could be very loud. Below are the expected answers.

(plane)	(butterfly)	(feather)	(alarm clock)
very loud	very quiet	very quiet	loud
(girl shouting)	(volcano)	(thunderstorm)	(mouse)
loud	very loud	very loud	quiet

2 **Think about it!**
The learner should be able to feel their throat moving; they may speak in terms of feeling their vocal cords vibrate.

Hear it and touch it

The learner should have completed the table following their observations. They should have a selection of objects and should have talked about touching some, hearing others and then describing the sensation. Try to accept any appropriate responses. Note that a plane can actually be heard and touched, but most children will rarely get to touch a plane. Some more examples are given.

What is it?	Can we hear it or touch it?	What does it feel or sound like?
a plane	hear it	very loud, like a motorbike
a doorbell	hear it	ding, ding, like a bell
a stone wall	touch it	hard, rough, cold to touch
a bucket of water	touch it	the bucket is cold and smooth, the water is wet and cool

4.2

Favourite salad foods

1 The learner should have drawn a salad food of their choice.

2 The learner should have completed the bar chart.

3 The learner should have looked at the bar chart and identified the favourite salad food.

4 The learner should have looked at the bar chart and identified the second most popular salad food.

Can you smell the sweet?

1. In the four boxes the learner should have referred to four stages in an investigation. There is some flexibility here as learners may break the investigation up differently. One example would be:
   - First I will find the equipment and write out my science question.
   - Then I will find four people and make a prediction.
   - Then I will test the people.
   - Then I will write the results and decide what I have found out.
2. The learner should have made a prediction.
3. In the space available the learner should have recorded the results in a table. What we are looking for is an effective record of results.
4. The learner should correctly identify, from their data, which flavour people could smell from the greatest distance.

4.3

Can we see to the side?

1. The learner will record the results of the sight test for three children.
2. The learner should conclude that humans can see a little to the side without turning their head.
3. **Think about it!**
   Very young human babies have poor eyesight. They are very well cared for and don't move around – they just need to be able to see their family.

5.2

Line up

Answers depend on the objects chosen.

Venn diagram

1. Answers depend on the objects chosen.
2. **Think about it!**
   Objects made from metal are often hard, strong, smooth, waterproof, shiny, rigid and grey or silver in colour. They conduct electricity and many are magnetic.

5.3

The strongest bridge

1. 3000 g
2. 3500 g
3. wooden bridge 2
4. paper bridge 2
5. wood
6. **Think about it!**
   Both metal and stone are used to make strong bridges.

5.4

Which paper is strongest when wet?

The learner should have carried out the activity and written the results in the table.

Draw a bar chart

2. Writing paper is strongest because it is less absorbent.
3. Toilet paper is weakest because it has to flush away easily.
4. **Think about it!**
   A paper towel needs to be strong when wet so that it does not tear easily when clearing up spilt liquids.

6 Forces and movement

6.1

Do the twist

1 and **2** The learner should have found, drawn and labelled objects that can be twisted and turned.

3 **Think about it!**
No, if you push on both sides of a bottle top it will not move. The lid will not turn.

6.3

Comparing weight

4 Answers will depend on objects used. Objects with more weight will make the rubber band longer.

5 Answers will depend on objects used. The height of the bar for each object should be equal to the length of the rubber band for that object.

6 **a** *When the rubber band is short, the weight is* smaller/less.

b *When the rubber band is long, the weight is* larger/bigger/greater.

c *The longer the rubber band, the* more weight the object has/heavier the object is.

6.5

Sliding coins

2 Answers will depend on surfaces used. The coin will slide less far on surfaces with more friction.

3 The answer will depend on the surfaces used. The surface with the most friction will be the one where the coin went the least distance.

4 The answer will depend on the surfaces used. The surface with the least friction will be the one where the coin went the furthest distance.

5 **Think about it!**
A surface with no friction would be very slippery. People might fall over. Objects would slide a very long distance before stopping.

Glossary

1 Looking after plants

absorb	to soak up liquid
cold	a temperature which is low
growth	the process of becoming larger and more developed
height	how tall something is
hot	a temperature which is high
leaves	part of the plant where the plant's food is produced
light	energy that comes from the Sun or a light bulb
measure	to find the size or amount of something, for example length or time
plant	a living thing that grows and has roots, a stem, leaves and often flowers
roots	parts of a plant that support the plant and collect water from the soil
temperature	how hot or cold something is
warm	a temperature between hot and cold
water	a clear liquid that all living things need to survive

Remember:

Practise saying these words aloud. Try to use them when talking about the topic.

2 Looking after ourselves

added salt	salt that is added to food before you buy it
added sugar	sugar that is added to food before you buy it
balanced diet	a diet with all the food groups but not too much or too little of any food
brain	your brain is where you think and know about the world around you; it also controls your body
breathe	to take air in and out of your lungs
carbohydrate	food that gives the human body energy
dairy	foods that have milk in them
exercise	moving around so that your heart beats faster
fat and sugar	we need a little fat and sugar but too much is bad for us
food group	foods are grouped by what they do to our bodies
fruit and vegetables	fruit and vegetables keep us healthy
healthy	good for your body
heart	your heart pumps blood around your body
kidneys	your kidneys help to clean your blood
muscles	your muscles can make your body move
nerves	nerves send messages around all your body.
oxygen	a gas found in the air that people need to breathe to live
plaque	a sticky substance on your teeth
predict	to think carefully about what might happen
protein	food that the human body uses for growth and repair, for example meat and fish
results	the observations or measurements made in a test
salt	small white crystals with a strong taste used in cooking
sugar	sweet white crystals we add to food and drinks
teeth	you use your teeth to chew food in your mouth
unhealthy	bad for your body

3 Living things

adult	an animal that is fully grown
Carroll diagram	a way of sorting data into a table
different	not the same
fingerprint	the lines on the tip of a finger
hibernate	spend the winter in a very deep sleep
invertebrate	an animal without a backbone
life cycle	the changes in the life of a living thing
life processes	things that all living things do
living	alive
non-living	not alive
observe	to look closely to find things out
question	a sentence that states what you would like to find out
record	to write or draw results to show what happened
similar	when things are the same in some ways but not exactly the same
sort	to put things into groups

4 Our five senses

bar chart	a chart that shows results using bars (the length of each bar shows the size of each result)
fair test	controlling a test by only changing one thing and keeping other things the same
hearing	the sense that uses your ears to hear
investigation	a test or experiment to find something out
sight	the sense that uses your eyes to see
smell	the sense that uses your nose to smell
taste	the sense that uses your tongue to taste
tongue	the part of your body you use to taste things
touch	the sense that uses your skin to feel

vibrate	small quick movements from side to side or up and down
vocal cords	the part of your body that vibrates to make your voice and other sounds; your vocal cords are at the top of your windpipe

5 Investigating materials

absorbent	a material that soaks up liquid
bridge	something that is built across a gap so that people can cross
flexible	can be bent
hard	not easy to squash, not soft
mass	the material a thing is made from and measured in grams and kilos
property	what something is like, for example a mirror is smooth and shiny
rigid	a rigid object keeps its shape, is not easy to bend or stretch, is not flexible
rough	feels bumpy to the touch
smooth	something that is flat, not bumpy
soft	a soft object is easy to squash, not hard
strong	hard to break or damage
Venn diagram	a way of sorting data using overlapping circles

Remember:

Practise saying these words aloud. Try to use them when talking about the topic.

6 Forces and movement

force	a push, a pull or a twist
forcemeter	something used to measure force
friction	the force between two objects when they rub together
gravity	a force that pulls everything down to the ground
pull	to use a force to move something towards you
push	to use a force to move something away from you
slide	to move across a smooth surface
surface	the outside part or top layer of something
turn	to move or make something move in a circle
twist	to turn an object about a fixed point
weight	the downwards force on an object because of gravity

Remember:

Practise saying these words aloud. Try to use them when talking about the topic.